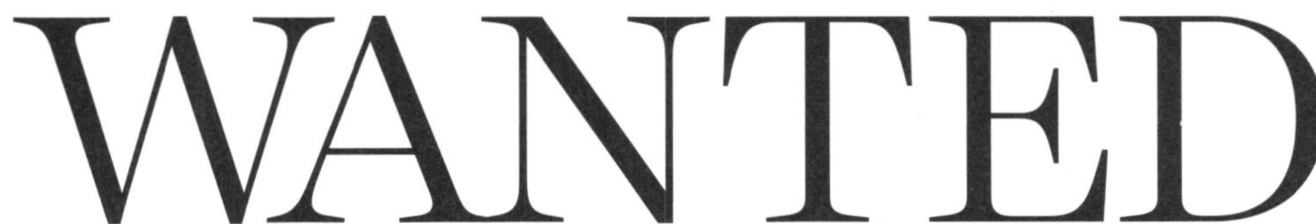

CAMAL PIRBHAI *and* CAMILLE TURNER

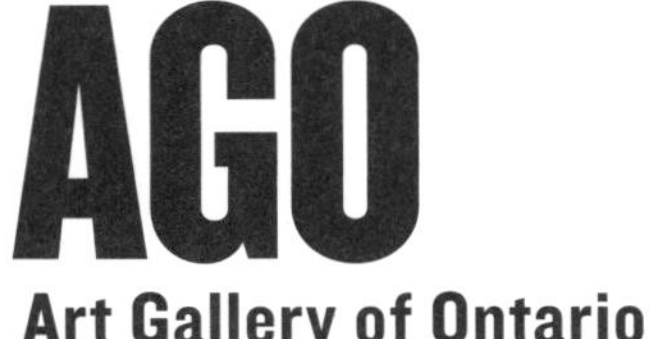

The 150th anniversary of Canada's confederation has provided us with an opportunity, but it was never our intent for these works to be viewed as historical documentation of the nation's past. It would have been easy to draw from a missing national narrative and simply expose these facts in a re-enactment, shedding light on a dark subject. As artists, however, Camille and I share a far deeper responsibility.

Our goal is to provoke a discussion that is relevant to our current times and more importantly, to manifest the vision we have for the future. It's too simplistic to look back and criticize or pass judgment. Explaining the ways in which the nation's past has shaped our current society is the job of historians and sociologists. We are looking for an audience to engage with this work on a more subconscious level. We consciously endeavour to speak to audiences who are not patrons of the arts, and who may not even be aware that they are looking at a piece of art.

We use fashion as a conduit for freedom. We place captions on our photographs directly copied from fugitive slave advertisements, and we use fashion as a tool to draw in unsuspecting viewers who may expect a branded promotional advertisement. Ultimately the goal is to slice through the layers of these works and arrive at a point of irony. Fashion may be our generation's hidden history. Will future generations comment on our current mythologies with the same distaste with which we regard our past? These images are part of our new narrative—an alternative truth, you might say. Isn't this the core of what art is?

—CAMAL PIRBHAI

When I moved to the Grange Park area near the Art Gallery of Ontario, I came face to face with historical silence. According to Michel-Rolph Trouillot, silences reflect power and are a byproduct of historical production.[1] Those who have the means to produce history also have the means to produce silence. Through Afua Cooper, a historian and writer, I came to understand that Black presence in the Grange Park neighbourhood actually dates back to 1793, when the town of York was founded. Some of the first Black residents of the area arrived as part of the military or as the property of white loyalists. This history was, until recently, largely unmarked and unacknowledged in official accounts of the area. Since then, I have made it my mission to un-silence the stories of the people of African descent who arrived here before me.

It has been my pleasure to work on the *Wanted* series with Camal Pirbhai. In this series of photographs, we address historical silencing by drawing on ads that were placed by Canadian slave owners in eighteenth century newspapers, when the people they enslaved had escaped. Using performers, we create images that seek to restore the humanity of people who were deemed property and excluded from Canada's historical narratives. We honour the courage they demonstrated through their resistance, and we strive to present them in ways that they must have imagined themselves, as people performing their right to freedom.

—CAMILLE TURNER

1. Michel-Rolph Trouillot, *Silencing the Past: Power and the Production of History* (Boston: Beacon Press, 1995).

Friendship,	John Richie,	—	Ditto.
Triton,	Thomas Byrne,	—	Ditto.

ADVERTISEMENTS.

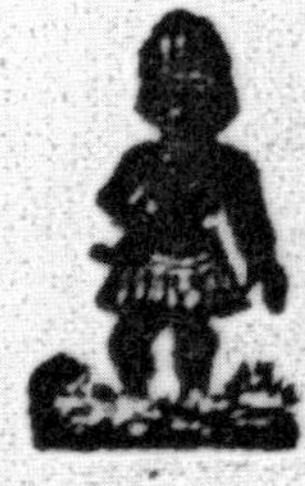

RUN away from Mr. GEORGE HIPPS on Thurſday laſt, a Mulatto wench named *BELL*, this is to give notice, that any perſon or perſons whatſoever who harbours the ſaid Girl may depend that he will go to the utmoſt rigour of the Law. When ſhe went away ſhe had upon her a Callico Gown and Petticoat, a dreſs'd Cap, and a black ſilk Handkerchief.

QUEBEC, *November* 3, 1778.

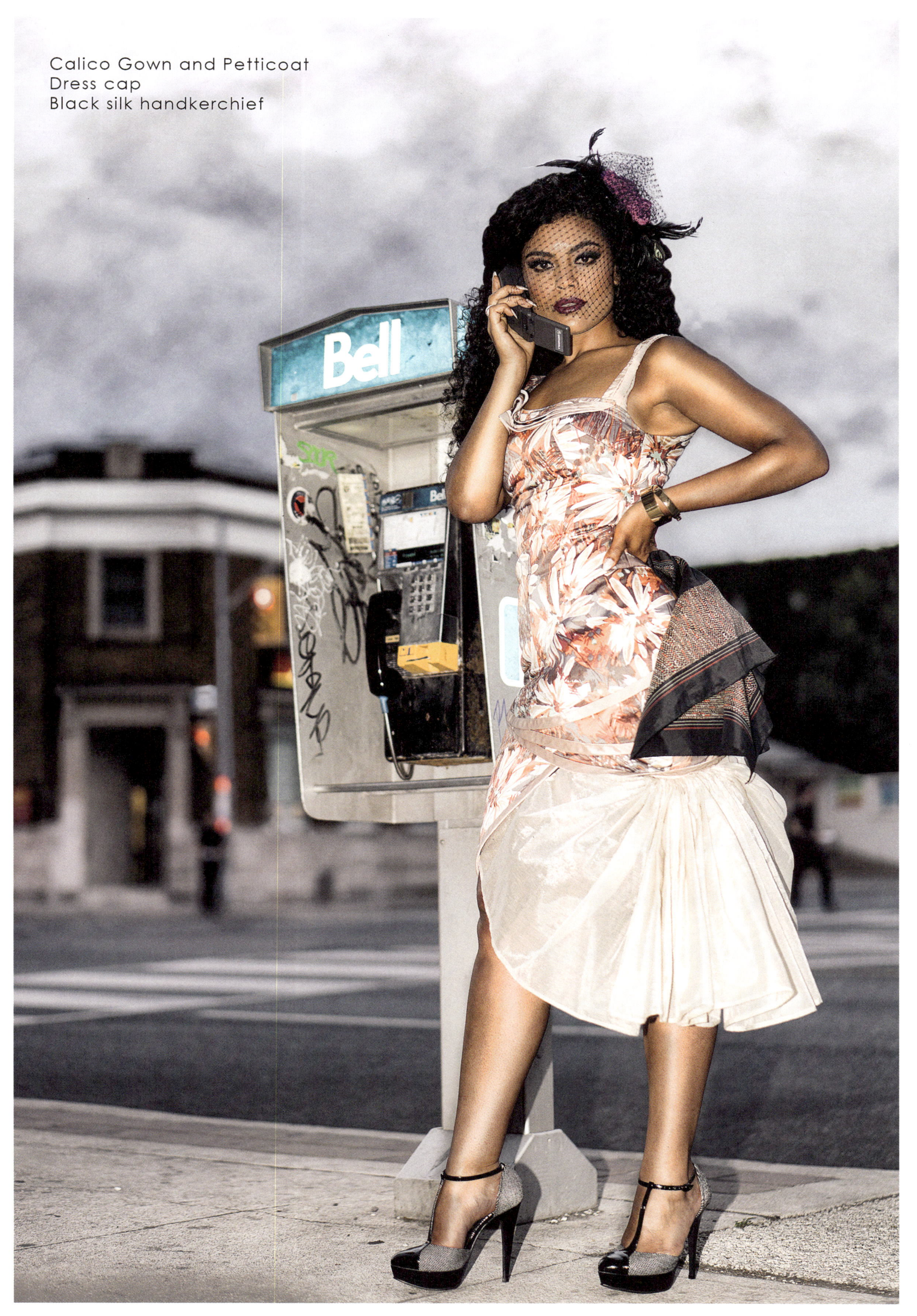

Calico Gown and Petticoat
Dress cap
Black silk handkerchief

RAN AWAY,

FROM the Subſcriber, on Thurſday the 31ſt Ult. a Negro Lad named CHARLES, about 20 years of age, four feet four or five inches high, with a white mark on the right ſide of his forehead; ſpeaks Engliſh and a little French and German; had on when he went away, a ſhort grey jacket, and large linen trowſers. Whoever will give information of him and put him again in my hands, ſhall have THREE GUINEAS Reward. PRE. GUEROUT.

Quebec, Auguſt 7, 1783.

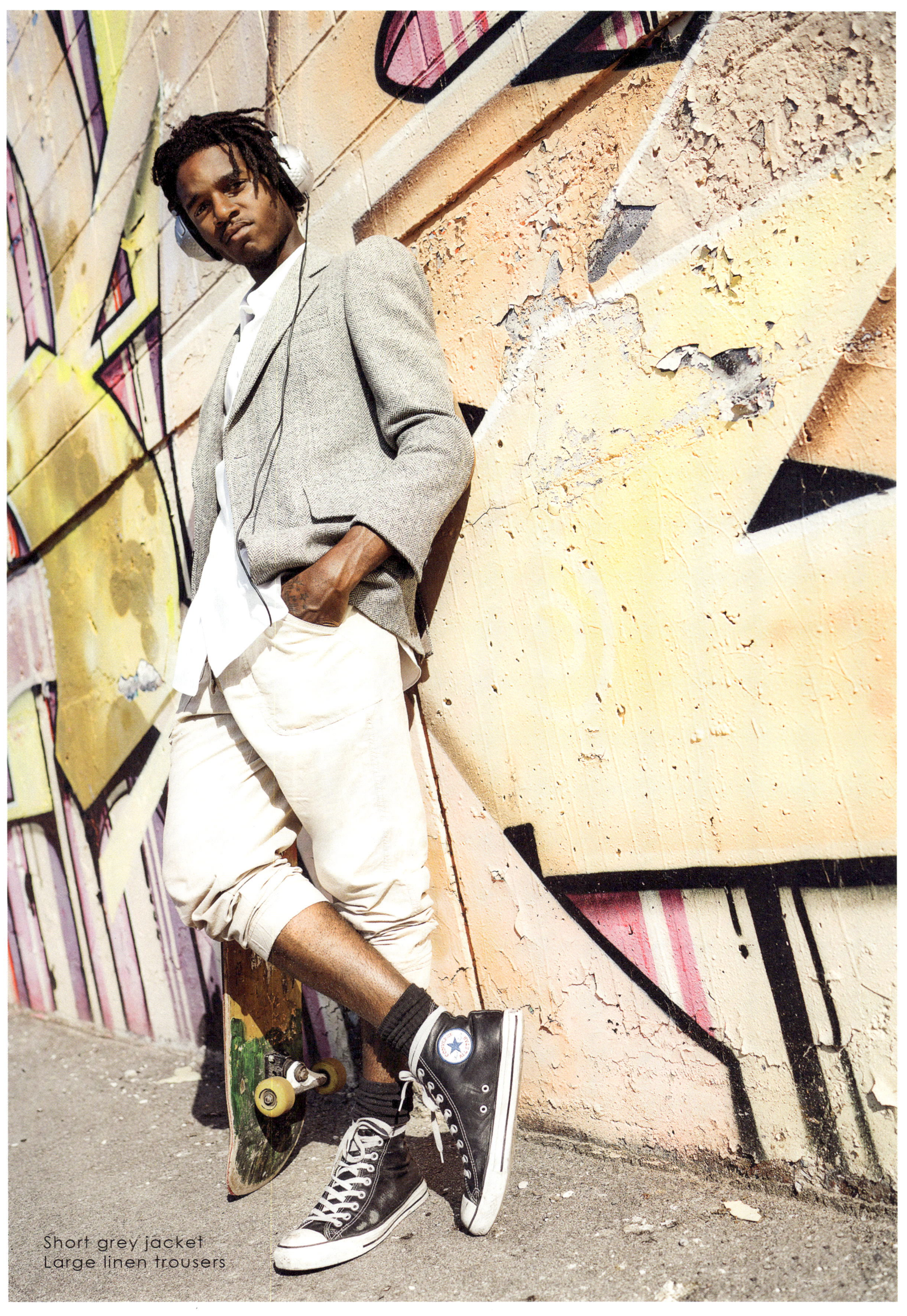

Short grey jacket
Large linen trousers

EIGHT DOLLARS REWARD.

RUN away from the Subſcriber on Saturday morning, a Negro man named ISHMAEL, aged about thirty-five years, five feet eight inches high, black ſhort curled hair, marked with the ſmall pox, wants ſome teeth, and a joint to his left hand little finger; ſpeaks Engliſh, a little French and Dutch; had on when he ran away a round hat, a ſailor's blue jacket, a white waiſtcoat, blue trouſers and no ſhoes, &c. It is ſuppoſed he will call himſelf a free Negro.

Whoever apprehends ſaid Negro, and brings him to his Maſter, ſhall receive the promiſed Reward, and all reaſonable Charges.

Montreal, 7th June, 1788. JOHN TURNER, Senior.

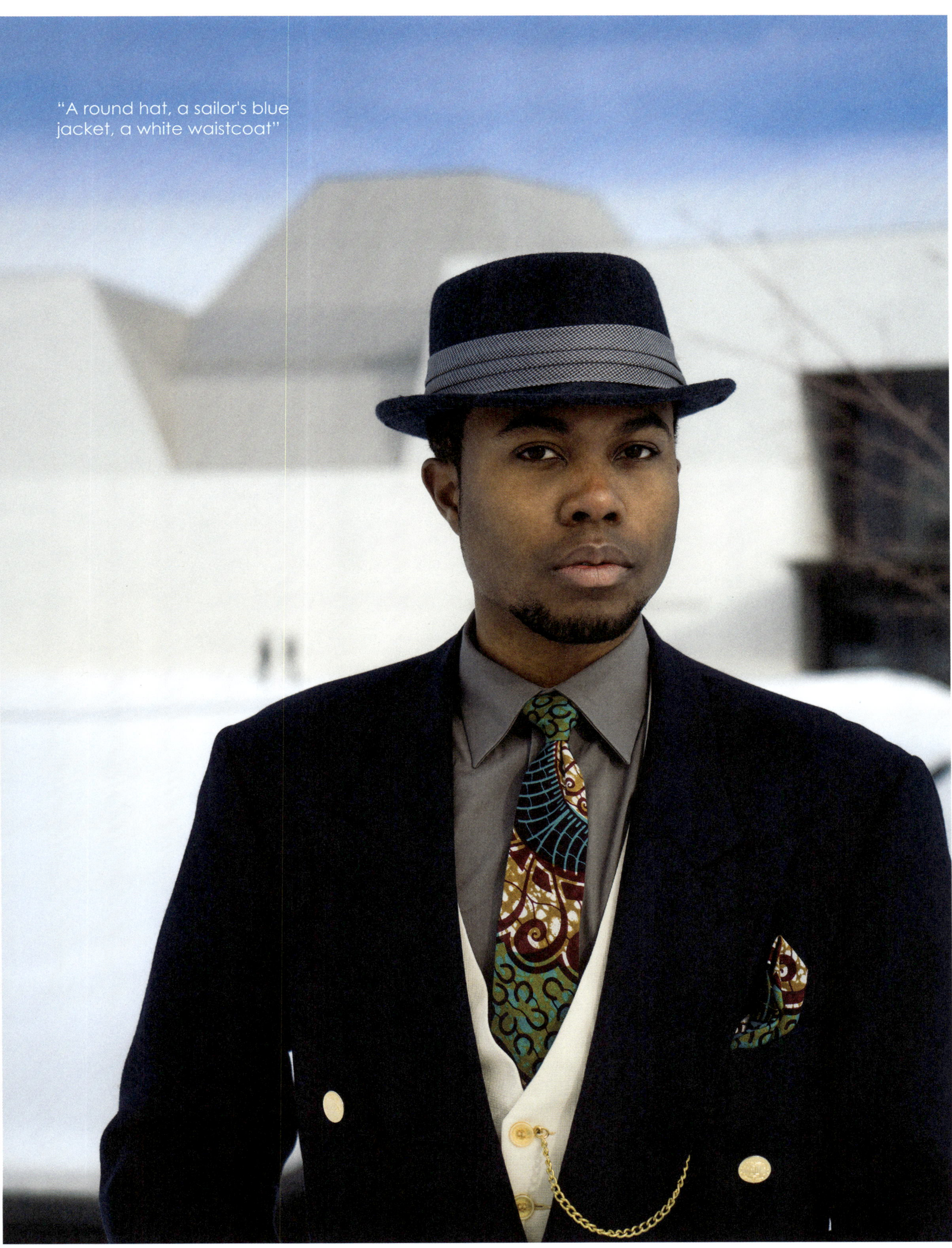
"A round hat, a sailor's blue
jacket, a white waistcoat"

Sign'd at Quebec, March 2d, 1784. *44th Regiment.*

FOURTEEN DOLLARS REWARD.

RUN-AWAY, on Sunday Night laſt, from the Subſcriber, a Negro-Man, named ISHMAEL, about 36 Years of Age, and nearly 5 Feet 6 Inches high; of a remarkably down-caſt Countenance, and a black and copper coloured mixt Complexion; his Hair is ſhort, ſtrong black and curly; and his Face much pitted with the ſmall Pox. He wants ſome of his Upper-fore Teeth, as likewiſe the firſt Joint of the fourth Finger of his left Hand; and beſides, on the middle of his Right-Leg, he has a freſh Eſchar from a Horſe Kick lately received and cured: had on when he went off, a round Hat cocked up behind and a blue ſilk Band; a red pluſh Waiſtcoat; a pair of blue Bath coating Leggings and Breeches in one; and a Pair of Shoes and Metal Buckles.

He came from Claverac near Albany in 1776, with his former Maſter, C. Spencer; can ſpeak and read Engliſh tolerably well, and underſtands a little Dutch and French: he paſſes himſelf, 'tis ſaid, as a Free Negro, the more eaſily to effect unoticed his intended Eſcape out of the Province. Whoever will apprehend the ſaid Negro-Man, and deliver him to the Subſcriber, Merchant, Montreal, ſhall receive the above Reward, and all reaſonable Charges, from JOHN TURNER.

Montreal, March 1, 1784.

TEN POUNDS REWARD.

"A round Hat cocked up behind and a blue Silk Band, a red push Waistcoat, a pair of blue Bath coating Leggings and Breeches in one and a pair of shoes and Metal Buckles"

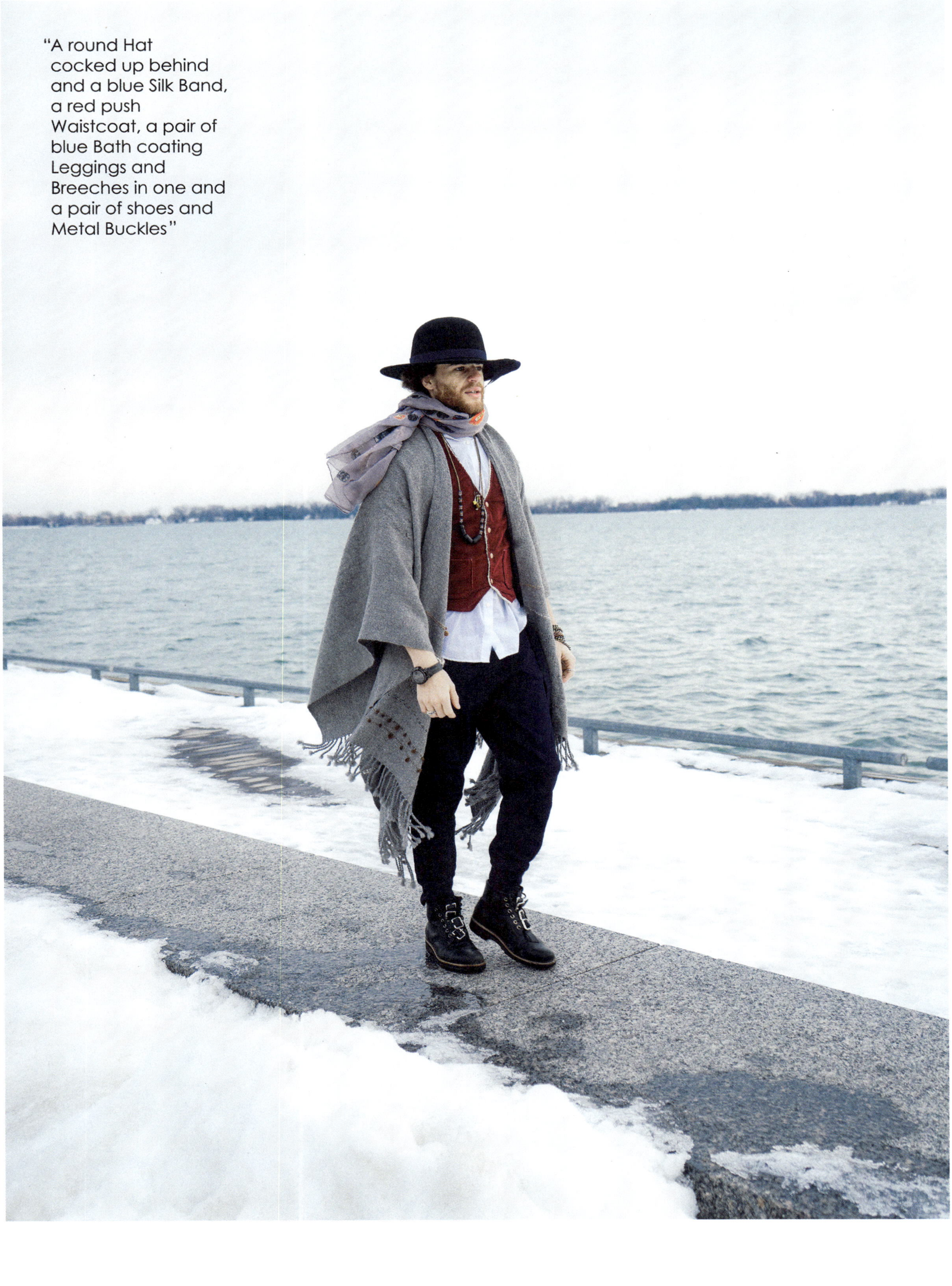

ADVERTISEMENTS.

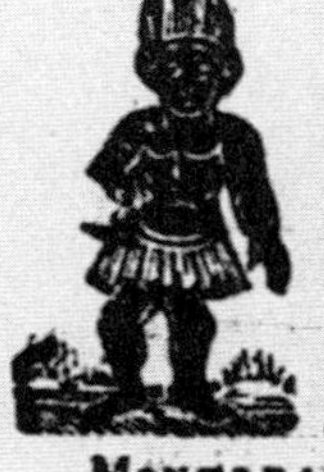

RUN AWAY on Saturday night the 10th Inſtant, a Negro man named JACK, about five feet eight inches high, had on when he went away a red coat faced with green, buff waiſtcoat and breeches, and an old blanket coat, ſpeaks no other tongue but Engliſh, and that upon the Guinea accent, his foretop turned back, very black, with a large beard, was lately purchaſed of Captain Covells, of Colonel Peters Volunteers. Whoever will ſecure the ſaid Negro, that his Maſter may get him again, ſhall have a Reward of EIGHT DOLLARS and all reaſonable charges paid by FINLAY & GREGORY, merchants near the Market-place Montreal.

MONTREAL, May 13, 1778.

IL s'eſt enfui Samedi la nuit, 10 du préſent, un Negre nommé JACK, d'environ cinq pieds huit pouces; lorſqu'il s'eſt enfuit il avoit un habit rouge, parmenté de verd, une paire de culottes et une veſte de buffle, et un vieil capot de couverte, il ne parle que langue Angloiſe, encore avec l'accent de la Guiné. Son toupet relevé, très noire avec beaucoup de barbe. Il a été dernierement acheté du Capitaine Covells des volontaires du Colonel Peters. Quiconque ramenera le dit Negre à ſon maitre, aura une récompenſe de HUIT PIASTRES, et il ſera rembourſé de tous ſes frais raiſonables par FINLAY & GREGORY, marchands près la place du marché de Montréal.

Montréal, le 13 Mai, 1778.

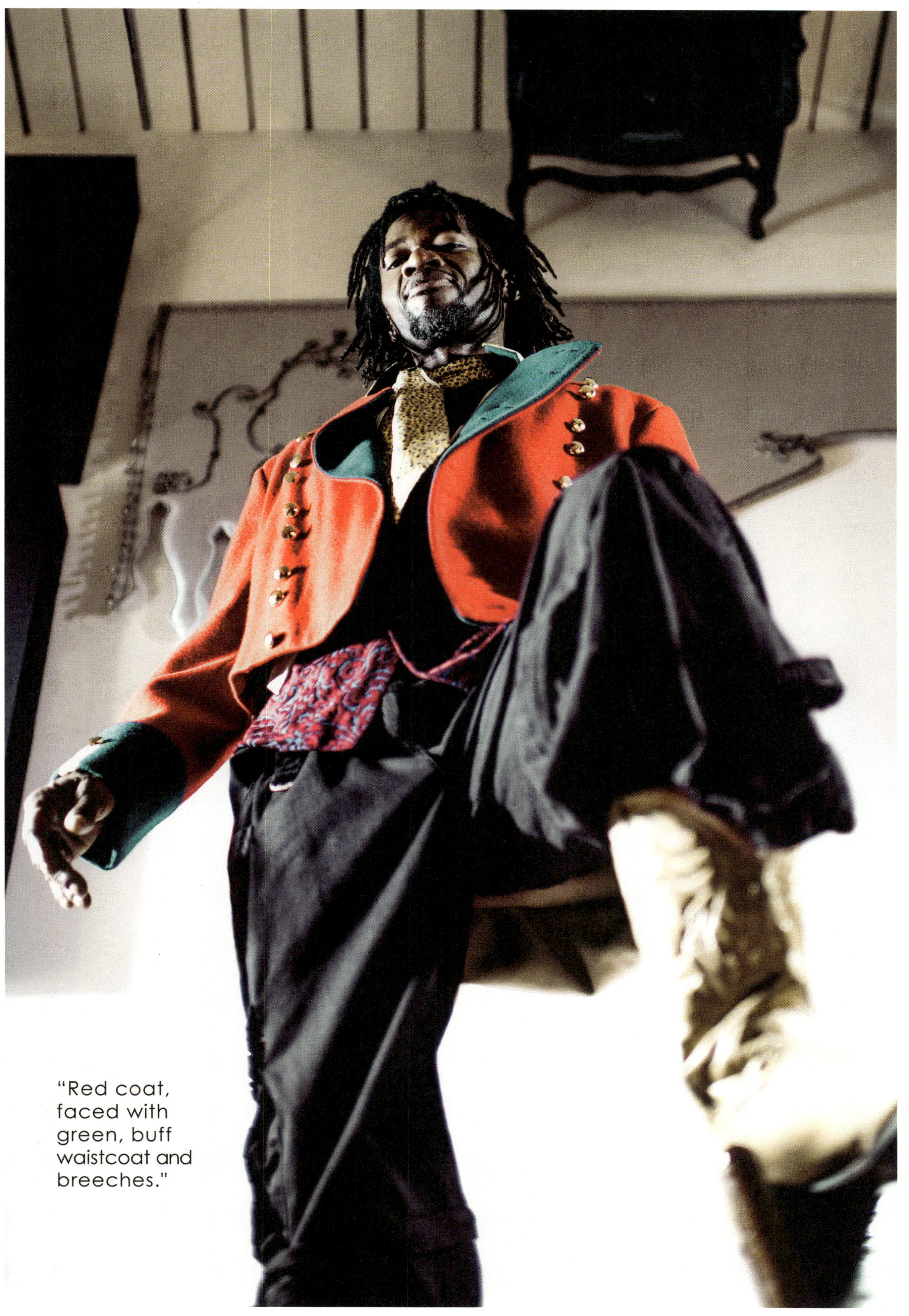

"Red coat, faced with green, buff waistcoat and breeches."

N. B. The ſubſcribers have alſo to let, that pleaſant Houſe on the hill, (either together or ſeparately) now occupied by Meſſrs. *Dorion*, and *Sarjeant*.

Quebec, 6th March, 1787.

RAN-AWAY from the ſubſcribers, between the hours of ſeven and eight o'clock yeſterday evening, a NEGRO WENCH named BETT, about eighteen years old, middle ſtature, ſpeaks the Engliſh, French and German languages well; had on when ſhe went away, a blue Kerſey Jacket and Pettycoat, a dark cotton Cap with yellow ſtrings, and an Indian Shawl round her neck, was big with child, and within a few days of her time.

Whoever will apprehend ſaid Negreſs, and ſecure her return, ſhall be paid A REWARD of TWENTY DOLLARS, and all reaſonable expences.

Any perſon who may harbour or conceal the ſaid Negreſs, will be proſecuted to the rigour of the law, by

JOHNSTON & PURSS.

For SALE *by* AUCTION *on the Premiſes,*

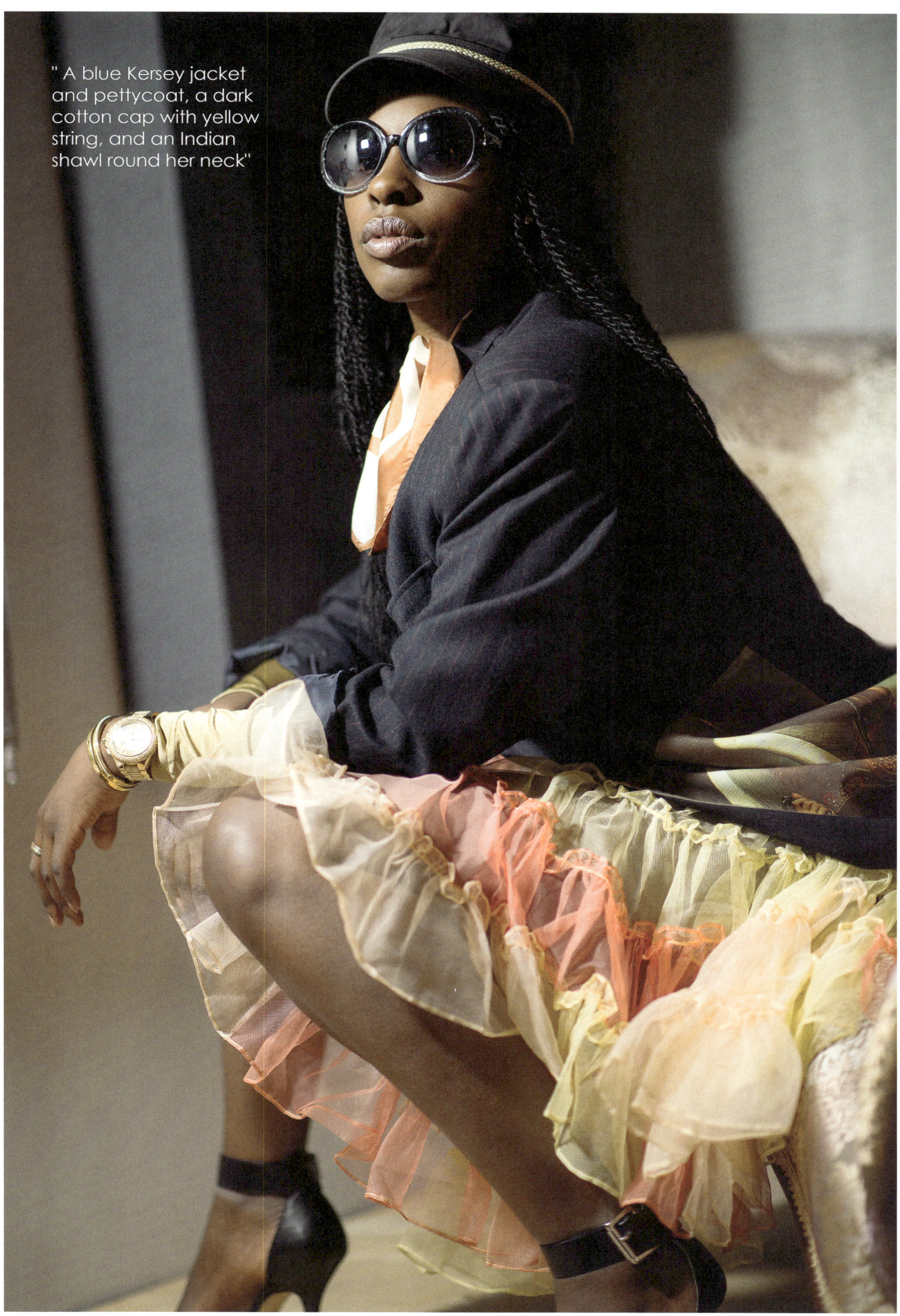
" A blue Kersey jacket
and pettycoat, a dark
cotton cap with yellow
string, and an Indian
shawl round her neck"

H. T. CRAMAHE.

RUN AWAY from the Subſcriber (on the Eighteenth Inſtant) a Negro man named *Lowcanes*, aged twenty-five Years, thin faced, and remarkable long hair tied behind, about five feet ten inches high, ſpeaks good French, no Engliſh, plays the Violin very well. He had on when he went off a light coloured ſhort coat with a red cape to it, waiſtcoat and breeches: Whoever ſecures the ſaid Negro man ſo that his Maſter may have him again ſhall have ſixteen Dollars reward, and charges from

22d November, 1775. WILLIAM GILL.

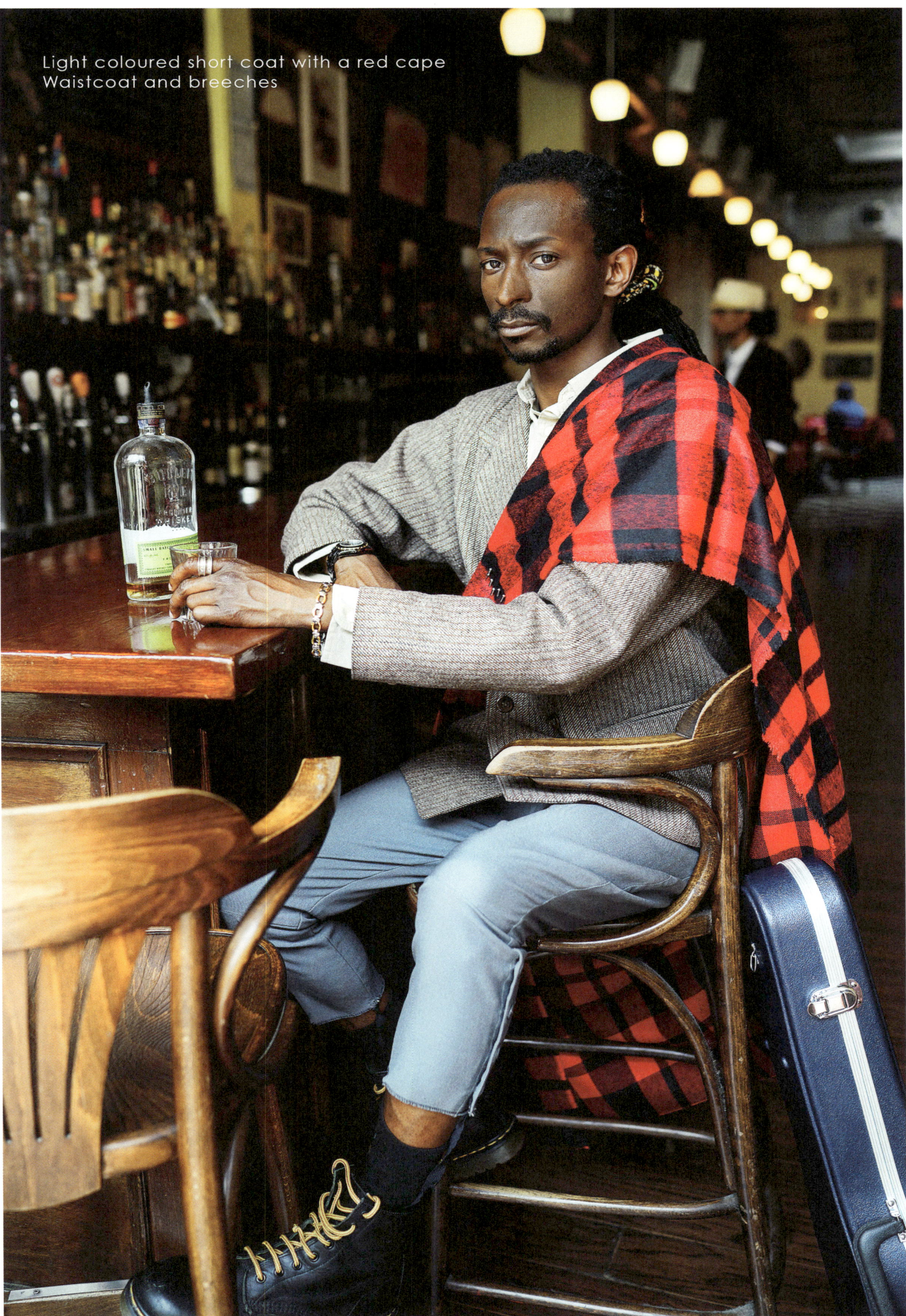

Light coloured short coat with a red cape
Waistcoat and breeches

RUN AWAY on Thurſday morning laſt from the Subſcriber, A Mullatto man Named Tom. Brooks, Aged Thirty years, about five feet eight Inches high, ſtrong made, had on a Mixed Brown Coat and Weaſtcoat, Green trowſers, a white Beaver hat with broad Gold-lace; ſpeaks Engliſh and French perfectly; was in Company with one Richaard Sutton by trade a Carpenter, who had on a Blue Jacket, a pair of white trowſers and new hat. Whoever Secures the ſaid Mullatto or Sutton, ſo that the Subſcriber may be informed of it, ſhall have a Reward of Five Pounds.

Robt. M. Guthrie.

Quebec Supt. 22d. 1785.

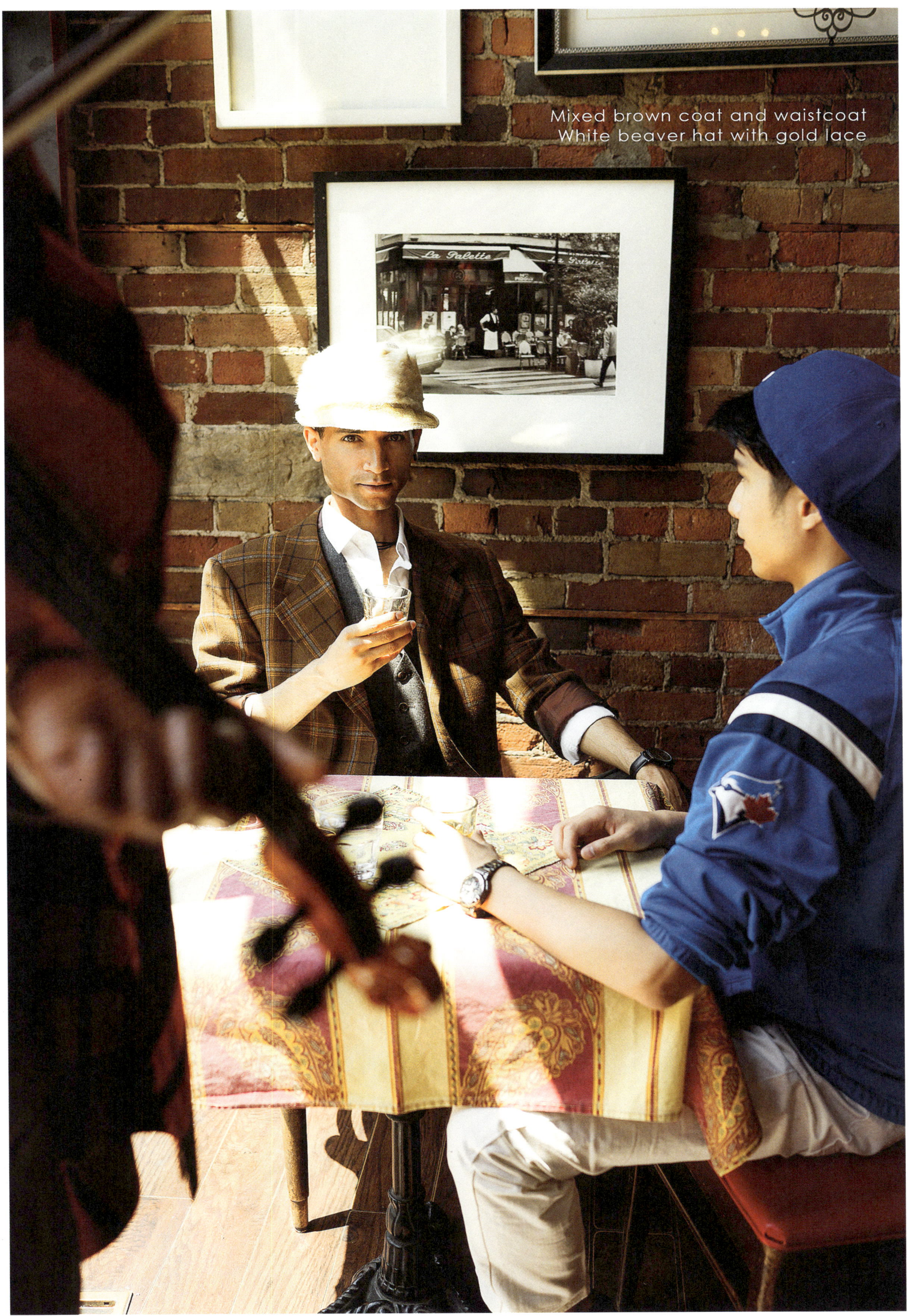

Mixed brown coat and waistcoat
White beaver hat with gold lace

RUN-AWAY, *on Saturday the 22d of August*, 1766,
from I. WERDEN, *in Quebec*,

A NEGRO GIRL, of about 24 Years of Age, pitted with the Small-pox, ſpeaks good Engliſh: Had on a black Gown and red Callimanco Petticoat; and ſuppos'd to have Caſh, both Gold and Silver, with her. Whoever apprehends ſaid Negro Girl, and brings her back to ſaid WERDEN, or to Mrs. *Mary Wiggans*, at Montreal, ſhall have ONE PISTOLE Reward, and all neceſſary Charges, paid by

I. WERDEN.

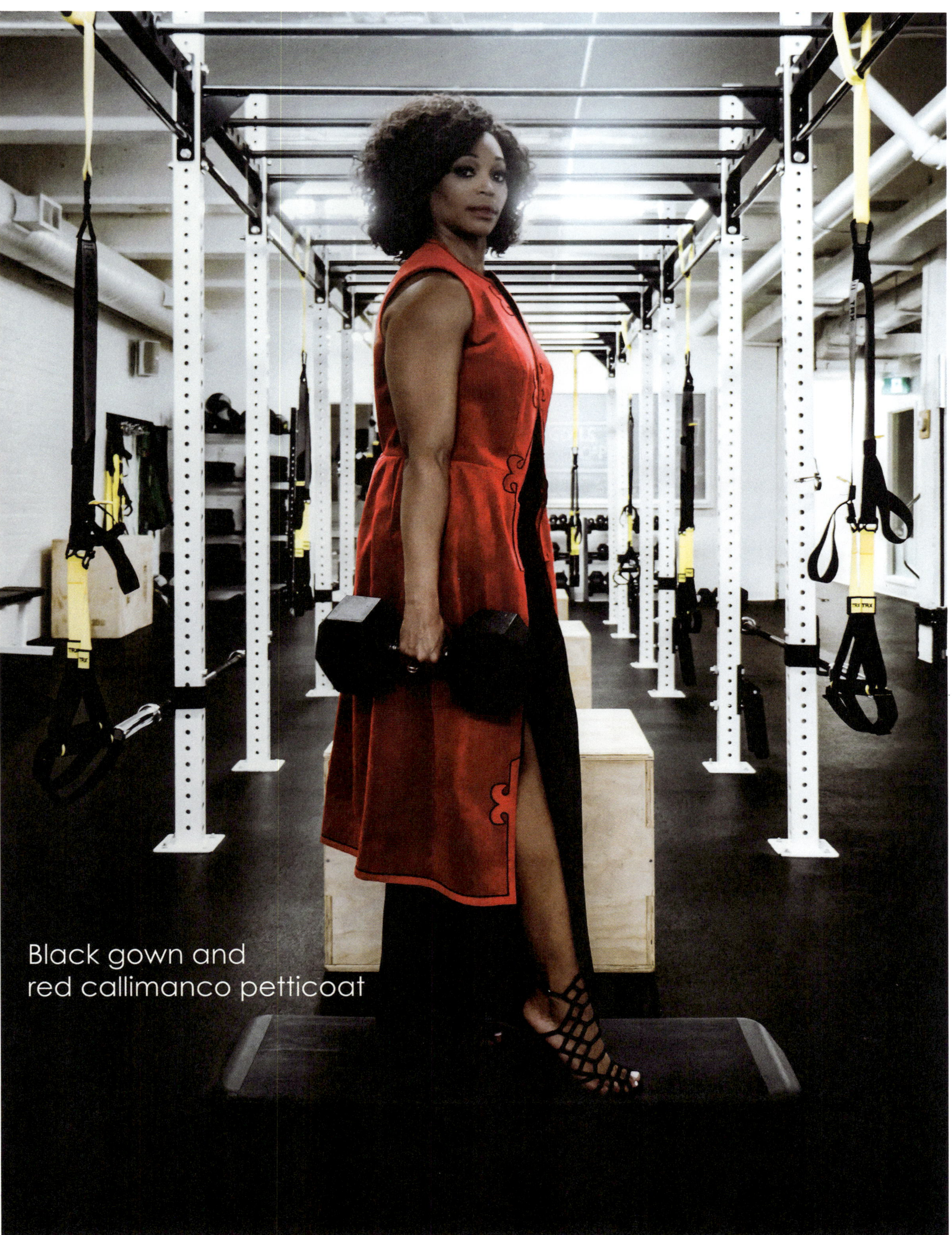

Black gown and
red callimanco petticoat

Hard Bread, &c. &c. &c.

RAN AWAY

FROM the subscriber living at the Nashwakshis, in the county of York, between the 15th and 21st days of this instant July, the following bound Negro slaves, viz. ISAAC about 30 years old, born on Long Island near New-York, had on when he went away, a short blue coat, round hat and white trowsers. BEN, about 35 years old, had on a Devonshire kersey jacket lined with Scotch plad, corduroy breeches, and round hat. FLORA, a Wench about 27 years old, much pitted with the small-pox, she had on a white cotton jacket and petticoat. ALSO NANCY about 24 years old, who took with her a Negro child about four years old called LIDGE. The four last mentioned Negroes were born in Maryland, and lately brought to this country.

ALL persons are hereby forbid to harbour any of the above Negroes, and all masters of vessels are forbid to take any of them on board their vessel as they shall answer the consequences. A REWARD of TWO GUINEAS, will be paid for each of the men, and SIX DOLLARS for each Negro woman, by Mr. THOMAS JENNINGS, if taken and deliver'd to him at the city of Saint John, at York Point, and if taken any where else and deliver'd to the said JENNINGS, or to the subscriber in York County, the like reward with all reasonable charges will be paid by the said JENNINGS or the subscriber.

CALEB JONES.

24th JUNE, 1786.

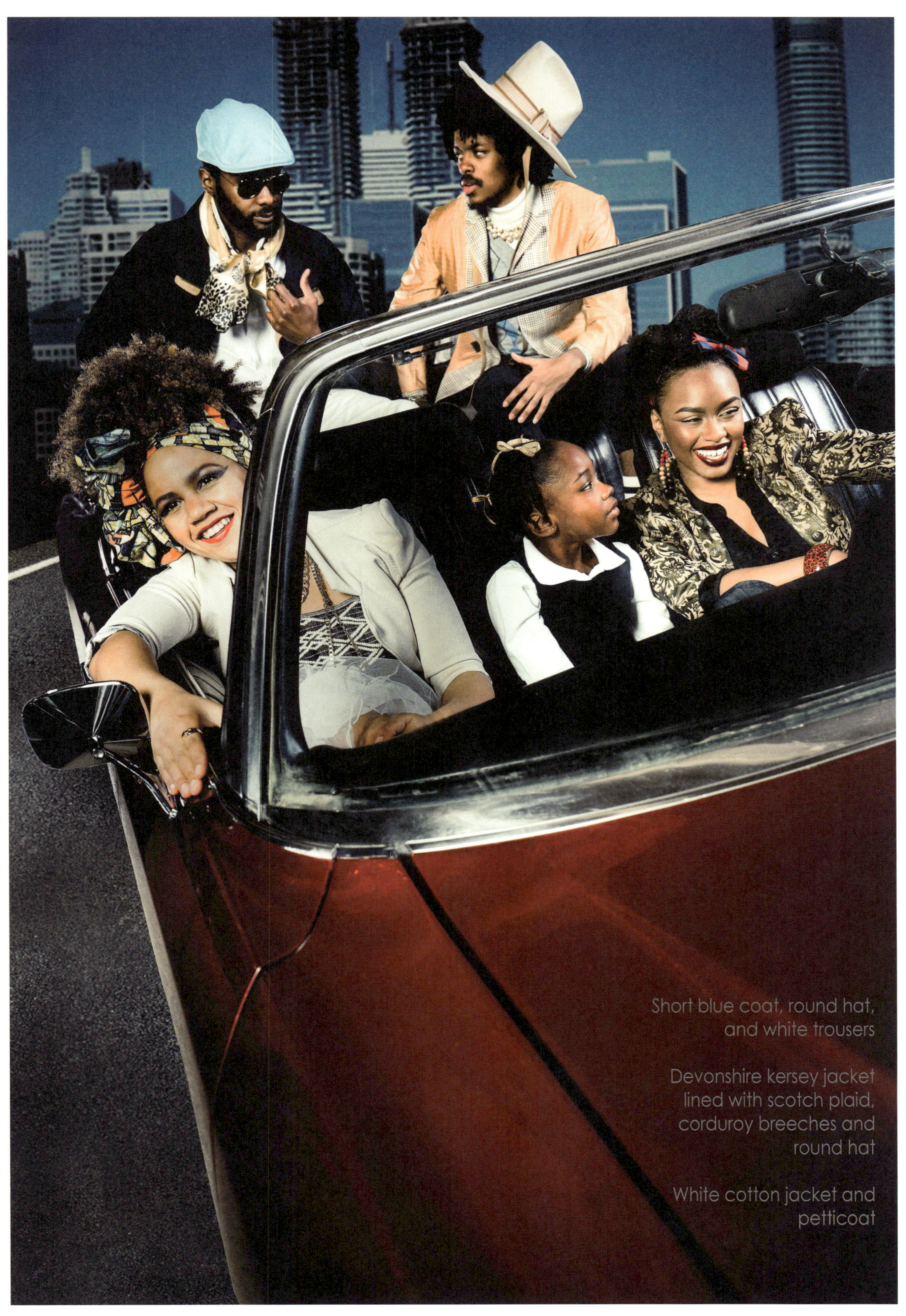

Short blue coat, round hat, and white trousers

Devonshire kersey jacket lined with scotch plaid, corduroy breeches and round hat

White cotton jacket and petticoat

Published in 2017 by the Art Gallery of Ontario. Copyright © 2017 Camal Pirbhai and Camille Turner, and the Art Gallery of Ontario.

The artwork in this publication was included in the Art Gallery of Ontario's exhibition *Every. Now. Then: Reframing Nationhood,* June 29, 2017–December 10, 2017, curated by Andrew Hunter with Anique Jordan and Quill Christie-Peters. The essay by Charmaine A. Nelson also appears in the *Every. Now. Then.* catalogue, published by the Art Gallery of Ontario in 2017.

EDITED BY
Andrew Hunter

MANAGING EDITOR
Jim Shedden

PRODUCTION EDITOR
Gina Badger

MANUSCRIPT EDITOR
Mosa McNeilly

COPY EDITOR
Amy Lam

DESIGN
The Office of Gilbert Li

PRE-PRESS
Type A Print Inc.

PRINTING AND BINDING
Friesens, Canada

Every effort has been made to trace ownership of visual and written material used in this book. Errors or omissions will be corrected in subsequent printings provided notification is sent to the publisher.

All rights reserved. No part of this publication may be reproduced, stored in a retrieval system or transmitted, in any form or by any means, without the prior written consent of the publisher or a licence from the Canadian Copyright Agency (Access Copyright). For a copyright licence, visit www.accesscopyright.ca or call 1-800-893-5777.

Printed and bound in Canada

10 9 8 7 6 5 4 3 2 1

A catalogue record for this publication is available from Library and Archives Canada

ISBN 978-1-894243-99-5

The Art Gallery of Ontario is partially funded by the Ontario Ministry of Culture. Additional operating support is received from the City of Toronto, the Department of Canadian Heritage and the Canada Council for the Arts.

Contemporary programming at the Art Gallery of Ontario is supported by

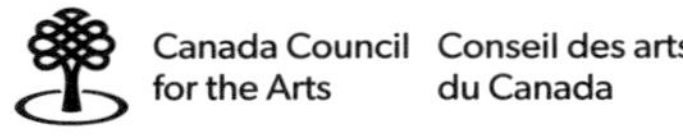

Every. Now. Then: Reframing Nationhood is organized by the Art Gallery of Ontario. This project is supported by government partners Ontario 150, the Government of Canada, and the Canada Council for the Arts.

Art Gallery of Ontario
317 Dundas Street West
Toronto, Ontario M5T 1G4
Canada
www.ago.ca

Wanted Series

ARTISTS
Camal Pirbhai
Camille Turner

PERFORMERS
Britta B. *as Flora* (group photo)
Kehinde Bah *as Lowcanes*
Kennedy Janae Douglas-Gannon *as Lidge* (group photo)
Tim Hunter *as Isaac* (group photo)
David Lewis-Peart *as Ishmael 1*
Desmond Miller *as Ishmael 2*
Tracy Moore *as Unnamed woman*
Chiedza Pasipanodya *as Bett*
Zaire Puil-Dalhouse *as Bell*
Kasia Smith *as Nancy* (group photo)
Stephen Surlin *as Tom*
Lee Turner *as Jack*
Jaleel Williams *as Charles*
Flimon Yohannes *as Ben* (group photo)

PHOTOGRAPHERS
Jalani Morgan
Christina Sideris

OTHER
Natasha Douglas
Bridget Faroo
Alvin Luong
Yasmine Mathurin
Jounghwa No
Andrea Pawson
Tracy Peart
Adilia Peres
Jovana Pirbhai
Memengwaans Sands
Trish Venema
GT Auto Works
La Palette

A very special thanks to Andrew Hunter, Anique Jordan and the whole AGO crew!

Conclusion

Returning to my original question, what is the meaning of such a deliberate re-imagination? Decked out in the most fashionable clothing, beautiful, charismatic, and self-possessed, these re-imagined subjects are no longer oppressed, frightened, hunted, and terrorized. They exude confidence, delight in frivolity, and embrace luxury—things not afforded their namesakes. By insisting that Bell, Bett, and Ishmael were not slaves, but *en*slaved—not possessions, but humans—we can see in their desire for freedom, as documented in their eighteenth-century fugitive notices, their heroism. This heroism resides not only in their literal quests for freedom but in their insistence that their bodies were their own, to be dressed (Thursday's red ribbon), styled, coiffed (Ishmael's cropped hair), and beautified as they—and not the slave owners—saw fit.

As Canadians reflect on the 150th anniversary of our nation, it behooves us to challenge the customary image of a homogeneously white Canada, one that strategically excludes the memory of Canadian participation in Transatlantic slavery and erases the centuries-long presence of people of African descent. Through the re-imagining of Bell, Bett, Ishmael, and other valiant freedom seekers, Camille Turner and Camal Pirbhai challenge us to think anew about the tremendous importance of integrating the memory and histories of Black Canada into our national narrative.

Dr. Charmaine A. Nelson holds a Ph.D. in Art History from the University of Manchester. A professor at McGill University, she lives in Montreal. Her book Slavery, Geography, and Empire in Nineteenth-Century Marine Landscapes of Montreal and Jamaica *was published in 2016.*

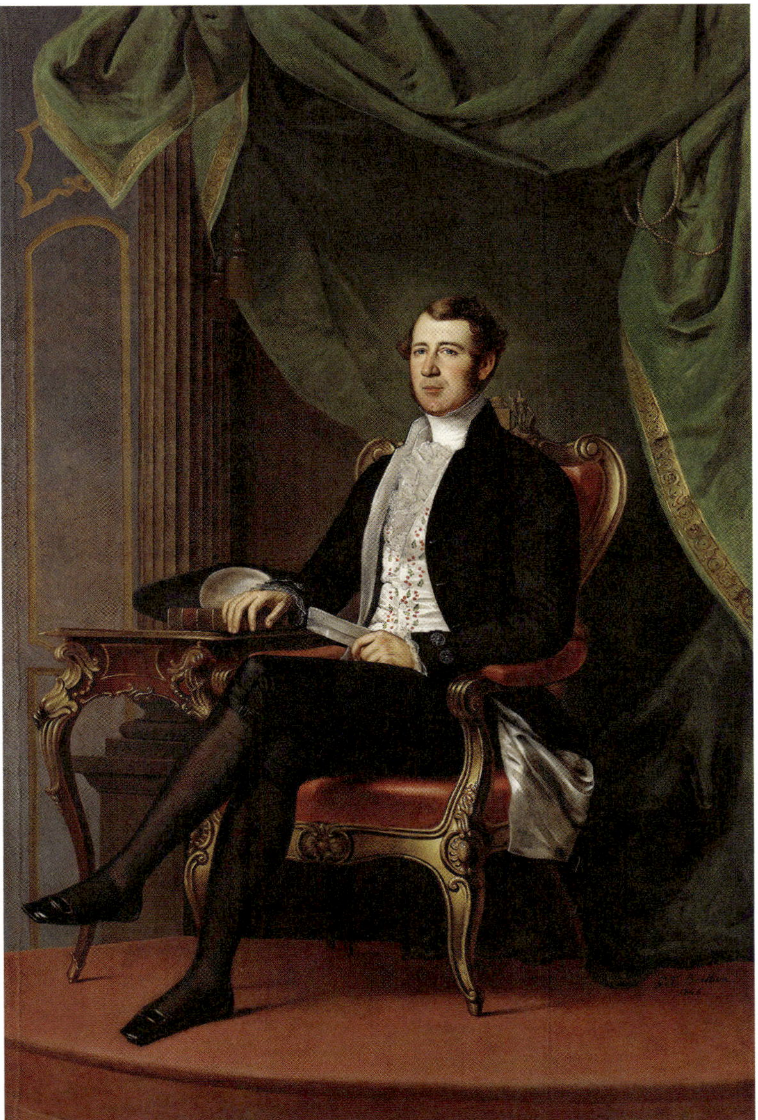

NOTES

1. "Heritage minutes: Underground railroad," *Historica Canada* website, video; released 1991. The focus on Canada as a land of abolitionism only, has been assisted by the circulation of popular representations like "Heritage Minutes: Underground Railroad."

2. George Hipps, "RAN AWAY from my service," *Quebec Gazette,* August 20, 1778; and, "RUN away from Mr George Hipps," *Quebec Gazette,* November 5, 1778; reproduced in Frank Mackey, "Appendix I: Newspaper Notices," in *Done with Slavery: The Black Fact in Montreal, 1760–1840* (Montreal: McGill-Queen's University Press, 2010), 321.

3. James Johnston and John Purss, "RAN-AWAY from the subscribers," *Quebec Gazette,* March 8, 1787; in Mackey, "Appendix I: Newspaper Notices," 329.

4. I am grateful to Sylvia Hamilton for sharing with me her idea of enslaved fugitives as freedom-runners; conversation between Sylvia Hamilton and the author, November 7, 2015, Halifax, Nova Scotia.

5. Graham White and Shane White, "Slave Hair and African American Culture in the Eighteenth and Nineteenth Centuries," *Journal of Southern History,* 61, no. 1 (February 1995): 49.

6. Laird W. Bergad, *The Comparative Histories of Slavery in Brazil, Cuba, and the United States* (Cambridge: Cambridge University Press, 2007), xiii. Two places where the fugitive slave archive may pale in comparison to photographic archives of the enslaved are Cuba and Brazil, where slavery was not abolished until 1886 and 1888 respectively. For more on photography of the enslaved in Brazil see Margrit Prussat, "Icons of Slavery: Black Brazil in Nineteenth-Century Photography and Image Art," *Living History: Encountering the Memory of the Heirs of Slavery,* ed. Ana Lucia Araujo (Newcastle upon Tyne: Cambridge Scholars Publishing, 2009).

7. Ira Berlin, "From Creole to African: Atlantic Creoles and the Origins of African-American Society in Mainland North America," *William and Mary Quarterly,* Third Series, 53, no. 2 (April 1996): 251–52. The Virginia planter, Robert "King" Carter (the richest planter in the state), who owned a plantation on the Rappahannock River, instructed his overseer to initiate a process of renaming his enslaved Africans at the point of purchase.

8. Marcus Wood, "Rhetoric and the Runaway: The Iconography of Slave Escape in England and America," in *Blind Memory: Visual Representations of Slavery in England and America, 1780–1865* (Manchester: Manchester University Press, 2000), 87.

9. John Turner, "FOURTEEN DOLLARS reward, RUN-AWAY, on Sunday night last," *Quebec Gazette,* March 11, 1784, in Mackey, "Appendix I: Newspaper Notices," 326.

10. Ibid.

11. Turner, "TEN DOLLARS REWARD," *Quebec Gazette,* July 29, 1779; in Mackey, "Appendix I: Newspaper Notices," 322.

12. Ibid., 321. The particular phrasing of this statement is also important because it discloses that black males wore wigs at this juncture. A later advertisement for the capture of "a Negro" William Spencer noted that he wore "a round hat and generally a wig." Jacob Kuhn and EDW. WM. Gray, "BROKE goal and escaped on Sunday the 18th," *Montreal Gazette,* November 22, 1792; in Mackey, "Appendix I: Newspaper Notices," 335.

13. Turner, "FOURTEEN DOLLARS reward," in Mackey, "Appendix I: Newspaper Notices," 326.

14. John Turner, Senior, "RUN away from the subscriber," *Quebec Gazette,* June 26, 1788; in Mackey, "Appendix I: Newspaper Notices," 331. Ishmael's dramatic change in hairstyle may have been a tactic to evade recapture, but equally, since African haircare was largely communal, the shorter hair may have been a practical consideration for a man enslaved in a slave minority community.

15. Trevor Burnard, "The Sexual Life of an Eighteenth-Century Jamaican Slave Overseer," in *Sex and Sexuality in Early America,* ed. Merril D. Smith (New York: New York University Press, 1998), 165.

16. Wood, "Rhetoric and the Runaway," 79.

17. Ibid., 82.

FIG 10 George Theodore Berthon, *Portrait of William Henry Boulton,* 1846. Oil on canvas, 240.5 × 147.5 cm. Collection of the Art Gallery of Ontario, The Goldwin Smith Collection, GS111.

Reading the Runaway

> FOURTEEN DOLLARS Reward
> RUN-AWAY, on Sunday Night last [28 Feb.] . . . a Negro-Man, named ISHMAEL, about 36 Years of Age, and nearly 5 Feet 6 Inches high . . . his Face much pitted with the small Pox. He wants some of his Upper-fore Teeth, as likewise the first Joint of the fourth Finger of his left Hand; and besides, on the middle of his Right-Leg, he has a fresh Eschar from a Horse Kick lately received and cured.[9]

Ishmael, twice represented by Turner and Pirbhai, ran away from the Quebec City merchant John Turner Sr. at least three times: in July 1779, March 1784, and June 1788 (Figure 7). Re-imagined as a dignified modern-day dandy (Figure 8) and a dignified cape-wearing gentleman (Figure 9), his scarred, marked, disabled, and no doubt abused body has been represented as that of self-assured, confident men. While John Turner described Ishmael as possessing a "black and copper coloured mixt Complexion," the modern-day Ishmaels emerge in two decidedly distinct hues—a move that challenges the authority with which whites laid claim to a knowledge of black bodies.[10] Gone is the "old Hat bedawbed with white Paint" (1779) and the pox-marked face.[11] Instead, the twenty-first-century Ishmaels exude confidence as both composure and self-possession.

While the most obvious glimpse of the original eighteenth-century Ishmael's ability to take control of his appearance arguably resides in the change in John Turner's description of his hairstyle—from "wears his own Hair which is black, long and curly" (1779),[12] to "his Hair is short, strong black and curly" (1784),[13] and finally to "black short curled hair" (1788)—the portraits of the re-imagined Ishmaels leave no doubt about who controls their likenesses.[14] Although Turner and Pirbhai are staging our epic re-encounters with enslaved freedom fighters, their fashionable, confident namesakes appear to have more in common with models in contemporary fashion magazines than with the enslaved people who navigated what Trevor Burnard has called "radical uncertainty."[15] The power of this potential reincarnation is that it allows us to think not only about what John Turner stole from Ishmael (his labour, years of his life, his access to self-determination), and how John Turner imagined and wanted to see Ishmael, but also how Ishmael, liberated from bondage, may have imagined and represented himself.

Fugitive Slave Advertisements as Portraits

What is called for is a rereading of fugitive slave advertisements not as mere texts but as *portraits,* however questionable, that function primarily through vision. However, the reconceptualization of fugitive slave advertisements as portraits of the enslaved is not a seamless fit for several reasons. First, while traditional "high" art portraiture—like that produced in marble or oil paint—was the end-product of a contract between a patron and an artist for a *flattering* likeness, the representations of enslaved fugitives generated by slave owners were designed to normalize slavery and to criminalize the enslaved for what Marcus Wood has termed "an act of theft, albeit a paradoxical self-theft"[16] (Figure 10).

Second, while in the traditional relationship the sitter and the patron were often one and the same, with fugitive notices the slave owner was the patron and creator of the notice, and the sitter was an unwilling participant in their representation. Third, while the artistic term for the represented subject in a portrait—the sitter—expresses the stillness required in the actual process of capturing a human likeness, a fugitive's escape was characterized by their self-directed motion, something that was literally coded as illegal under colonial law. Therefore, the portrait of the enslaved person that a fugitive slave advertisement captured was not of a stationary person—a sitter—but instead, of a person in motion, a runner.

Finally, since a fugitive's likeness was published against their will, these portraits were "stolen" and unauthorized. Yet they were also "fugitive" in the sense that they were elusive and often highly false images. They were false in the sense that slave owners deliberately vilified the character of the enslaved in the advertisements they placed, and could often not comprehend or accurately describe the African cultural practices of the enslaved. Furthermore, the commonality of fugitive tactics—like altering one's appearance or changing clothing to "pass" as another social group (mainly free people) in an age when most poor people had only one set of clothing—meant that the enslaved often did not precisely match their descriptions.

The medium of these printed portraits was text, as opposed to images, but the words were often strategically deployed with the goal of creating a mental image of the enslaved. Besides the height, weight, and clothing of the fugitive, such notices regularly recounted bodily marks. Ishmael is a case in point. The legalization of corporal punishment within colonial law meant that the bodies of the enslaved were commonly riddled with signs of violence. But the exposure of slave-owner violence in the description of the enslaved person's injured and tortured body—seen as necessary to the economic ends of the advertisement—signalled the moment in which the fugitive notice became a weapon against the slave-owning classes. As Wood explains, "the runaway emerges as a metaphor for white moral failure."[17]

FIG 7 Fugitive notice for Ishmael, placed by John Turner in the *Quebec Gazette,* March 11, 1784.

FIG 8 Camal Pirbhai and Camille Turner, *Ishmael,* from the *Wanted* series, 2017. Courtesy of the artists.

FIG 9 Camal Pirbhai and Camille Turner, *Ishmael,* from the *Wanted* series, 2017. Courtesy of the artists.

Sign'd at Quebec, March 2d, 1784. *44th Regiment.*

FOURTEEN DOLLARS REWARD.

RUN-AWAY, on Sunday Night laſt, from the Subſcriber, a Negro-Man, named ISHMAEL, about 36 Years of Age, and nearly 5 Feet 6 Inches high; of a remarkably down-caſt Countenance, and a black and copper coloured mixt Complexion; his Hair is ſhort, ſtrong black and curly; and his Face much pitted with the ſmall Pox. He wants ſome of his Upper-fore Teeth, as likewiſe the firſt Joint of the fourth Finger of his left Hand; and beſides, on the middle of his Right-Leg, he has a freſh Eſchar from a Horſe Kick lately received and cured: had on when he went off, a round Hat cocked up behind and a blue ſilk Band; a red pluſh Waiſtcoat; a pair of blue Bath coating Leggings and Breeches in one; and a Pair of Shoes and Metal Buckles.

He came from Claverac near Albany in 1776, with his former Maſter, C. Spencer; can ſpeak and read Engliſh tolerably well, and underſtands a little Dutch and French: he paſſes himſelf, 'tis ſaid, as a Free Negro, the more eaſily to effect unoticed his intended Eſcape out of the Province. Whoever will apprehend the ſaid Negro-Man, and deliver him to the Subſcriber, Merchant, Montreal, ſhall receive the above Reward, and all reaſonable Charges, from JOHN TURNER.

Montreal, March 1, 1784.

TEN POUNDS REWARD.

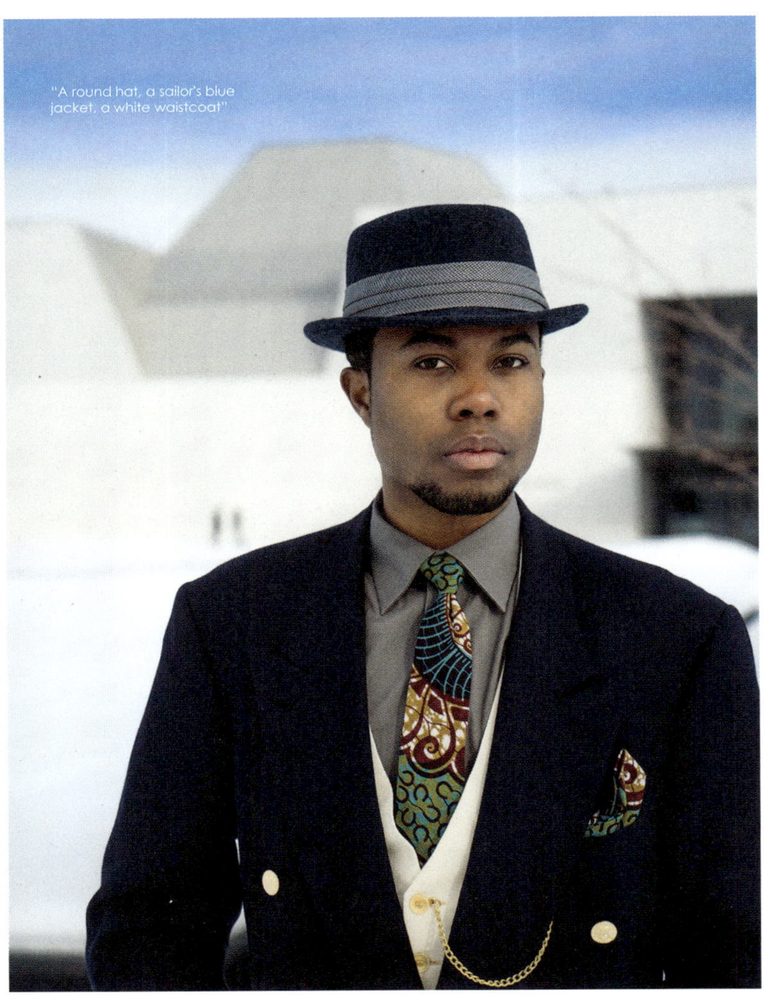

"A round hat, a sailor's blue jacket, a white waistcoat"

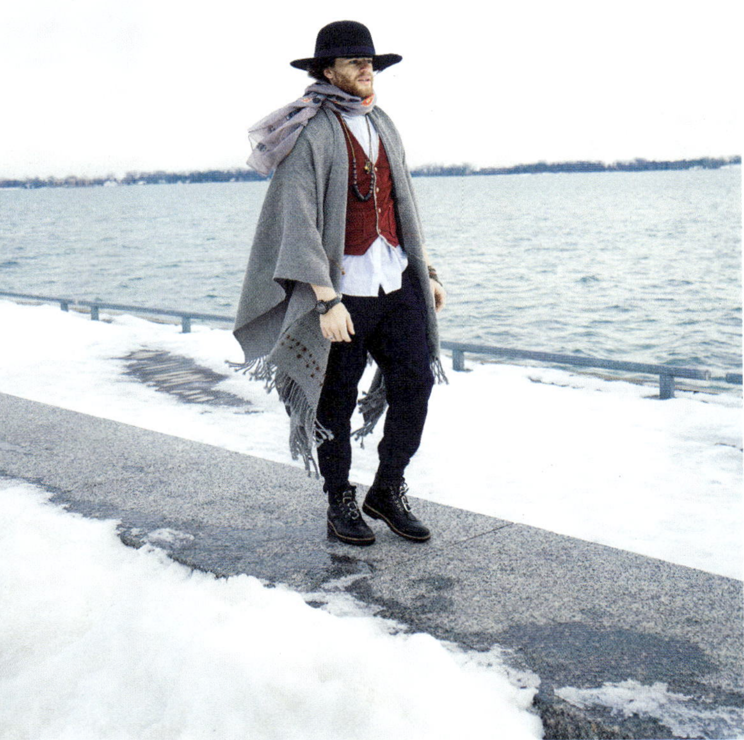

"A round Hat cocked up behind and a blue Silk Band, a red push Waistcoat, a pair of blue Bath coating Leggings and Breeches in one and a pair of shoes and Metal Buckles"

amuſement well directed Satire is ſure to give.

RAN AWAY from my ſervice, on Tueſday night the 18th inſtant, A Mulatto Negreſs named BELL. I do hereby promiſe a reward of FOUR DOLLARS to any perſon who will apprehend ſaid Negreſs and bring her to me, or lodge her in his Majeſty's gaol in Quebec. She wore when ſhe went away a ſtriped woollen jacket and petticoat, and had no ſhoes or ſtockings on. I do caution all perſons from harbouring ſaid Negreſs, as I am determined to puniſh any perſon in whoſe cuſtody ſhe may be found to the utmoſt rigour of the law.

QUEBEC, Auguſt 19, 1778. GEO: HIPPS.

Triton, Thomas Byrne, —— Ditto.

ADVERTISEMENTS.

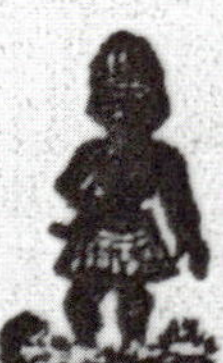

RUN away from Mr. GEORGE HIPPS on Thurſday laſt, a Mulatto wench named *BELL*, this is to give notice, that any perſon or perſons whatſoever who harbours the ſaid Girl may depend that he will go to the utmoſt rigour of the Law. When ſhe went away ſhe had upon her a Callico Gown and Petticoat, a dreſs'd Cap, and a black ſilk Handkerchief.

QUEBEC, *November* 3, 1778.

N. B. The ſubſcribers have alſo to let, that pleaſant Houſe on the hill, (either together or ſeparately) now occupied by Meſſrs. *Dorion* and *Sarjeant*.

Quebec, 6th March, 1787.

RAN-AWAY from the ſubſcribers, between the hours of ſeven and eight o'clock yeſterday evening, a NEGRO WENCH named BETT, about eighteen years old, middle ſtature, ſpeaks the Engliſh, French and German languages well; had on when ſhe went away, a blue Kerſey Jacket and Pettycoat, a dark cotton Cap with yellow ſtrings, and an Indian Shawl round her neck, was big with child, and within a few days of her time.

Whoever will apprehend ſaid Negreſs, and ſecure her return, ſhall be paid A REWARD of TWENTY DOLLARS, and all reaſonable expences.

Any perſon who may harbour or conceal the ſaid Negreſs, will be proſecuted to the rigour of the law, by JOHNSTON & PURSS.

For SALE *by* AUCTION *on the Premiſes,*

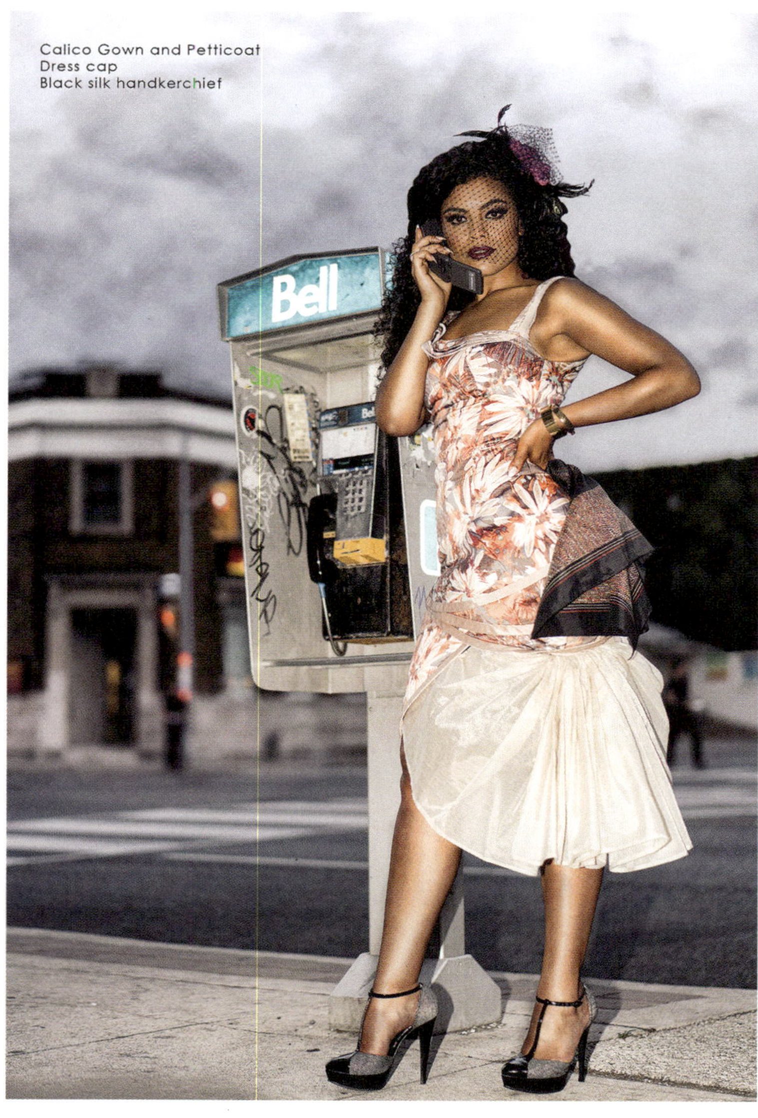

Calico Gown and Petticoat
Dress cap
Black silk handkerchief

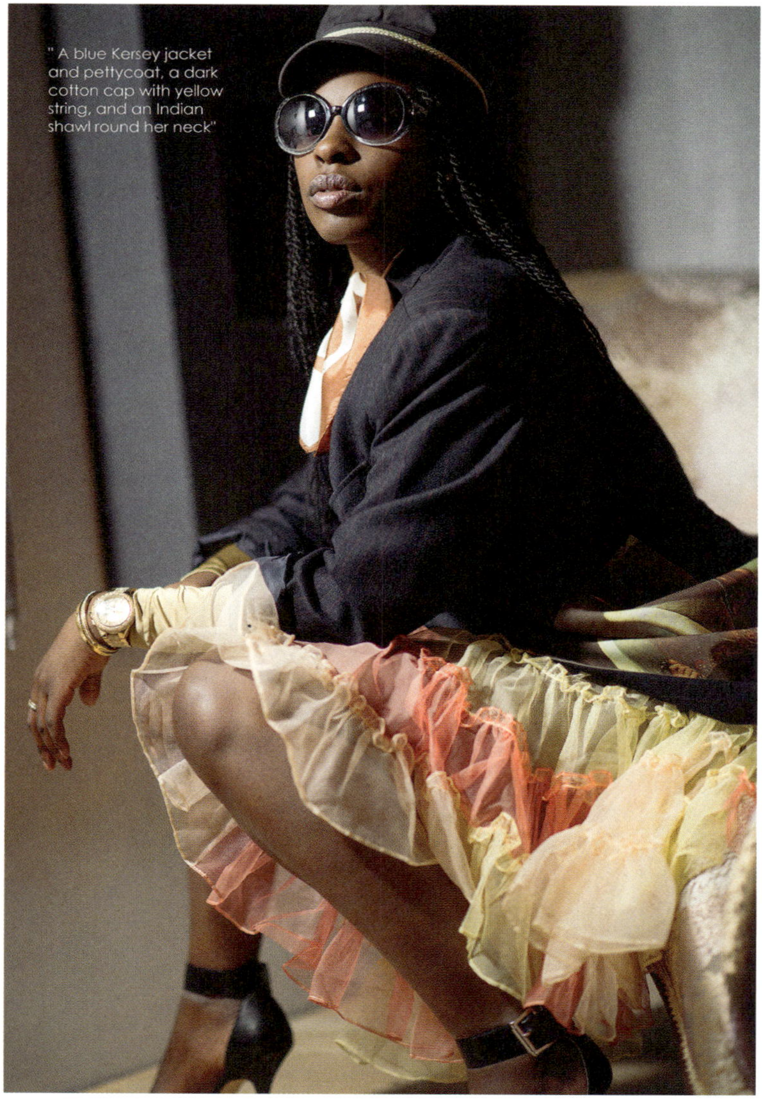

"A blue Kersey jacket and pettycoat, a dark cotton cap with yellow string, and an Indian shawl round her neck"

Since at least the seventeenth century, Africans arrived in Canada in bondage. Their forcible relocation from Africa, or other parts of the Americas, was facilitated by their designation, first as cargo, and subsequently as chattel; a strategy that excluded them from the category of settler. That these histories—spanning over two hundred years and two empires (British and French)—are overwhelmingly disavowed is a result of Canada's national myth of racial tolerance and, concomitantly, the profound failures of Canada's education system. However, it does not take much digging to uncover the lie of our blinkered, heroic, national self-aggrandizement as the territory to which enslaved African Americans fled.[1]

On Tuesday, September 1, 1772, John Rock of Halifax, Nova Scotia, placed a fugitive notice in the *Nova-Scotia Gazette and the Weekly Chronicle* for an enslaved Black girl known as Thursday (Figure 1). Rock's notice for Thursday obscenely juxtaposed descriptions of her self-care and beautification practices (the red ribbon worn about her head) with what was almost assuredly evidence of her physical abuse (the lump above her right eye). The fugitive notices placed for Bell and Bett, both of whom briefly escaped captivity in Quebec, also convey something of the specific horrors of female enslavement (Figures 2–4). Bell's two documented escapes, less than three months apart, attest to the urgency of her desire to flee.[2] That she first ran away in August 1778, with "no shoes or stocking on," and fled again in October 1778, when fall temperatures made escape even more perilous, speaks to her desperation. But the conditions of Bett's escape were even more dramatic. When the approximately eighteen-year-old Bett escaped on the winter evening of March 7, 1787, the merchants Johnston and Purss described her as "big with child, and within a few days of her time"[3] (Figure 4).

Fast-forward to 2017, and Bell and Bett have been re-imagined: Bell as a stunning, caramel-coloured vision in a figure-flattering dress and stiletto heels, her gaze confidently confronting us for daring to interrupt her mid-phone call; and the exquisite seated Bett, eyes concealed behind fashionable dark sunglasses, showing off her beautiful, chocolate-coloured legs beneath her multi-coloured, ruffled skirt (Figures 5 and 6). But what does it mean to re-imagine these eighteenth-century enslaved freedom seekers as poised and beautiful, twenty-first century divas?[4]

The colonial archive of fugitive slave advertisements (including significant collections in Nova Scotia, Quebec, and Ontario) calls us to understand the retention of African self-care practices within the world of psychic, physical, and social abuse and material deprivation that was Transatlantic slavery. Through their innovative photographic reinterpretations of enslaved Africans in Canada, Camille Turner and Camal Pirbhai exploit this archive to provoke a conversation about Canada's role in Transatlantic slavery, the stolen potential of our enslaved ancestors, and the resilience of Canada's diverse African populations.

The fugitive or runaway slave advertisement provides for us a window into the lives and worlds of the enslaved. Frequently printed in weekly newspapers alongside other news and advertisements of transatlantic significance, such notices routinely incentivized the public's cooperation with the offer of rewards and the threat of judicial retribution. Ubiquitous across the Americas, each example was about the recapture of an individual, or individuals, who had fled, and as such, required that their owners share details that illuminated what made the runaways unique, both in manner and appearance.

Research on the enslaved poses several substantial problems for the researcher; not the least among them are the ways in which the colonial nature of the archive occludes the lives of people who were held in bondage. Since the enslaved were considered cargo, commodities, or chattel in economic and legal discourses, white slave owners and their surrogates strategically prohibited them from being recorded in registries, ledgers, and documents, which were used to individualize and humanize whites.

Such advertisements are what Graham White and Shane White have referred to as "the most detailed descriptions of the bodies of enslaved African Americans available."[5] I would argue that their contention also generally applies to the regions of the Americas that practiced the Transatlantic slave trade, particularly places where abolition predated the development of photography.[6] Displaced from their homelands and forced to take up the role of un-free labour in the Americas, enslavement severely impeded the ability of Africans to remember their histories, maintain their ethnic specificity, practice their cultures, and care for their bodies. This was strategic on the part of white colonialists and the slave-owning classes, and evident in the immediate implementation of slave practices—like branding and renaming—that were meant to break the enslaved from their sense of individuality, family, and ancestry.[7]

Indeed, as Marcus Wood contends, "Slavery, as a legal and economic phenomenon, was premised upon the denial of personality, and of a personal history, to the slave."[8] Furthermore, ruling-class whites deliberately developed the colonial archive in ways that allowed Africans to enter almost always as the objects or "stock" owned by another, and therefore as partial and incomplete entries. This disturbing fact—that the most detailed representations of the enslaved were produced by their owners—provokes a confrontation with the archive, not as an objective or neutral container of facts and information, but as a site through which the elite secured their power by determining who could be represented and in what fashion.

FIG 2 Fugitive notice for Bell, placed by Geo. Hipps in the *Quebec Gazette*, August 20, 1778.

FIG 3 Fugitive notice for Bell, placed by Geo. Hipps in the *Quebec Gazette*, November 5, 1778.

FIG 4 Fugitive notice for Bett, placed by Johnston and Purss in the *Quebec Gazette*, March 8, 1787.

FIG 5 Camal Pirbhai and Camille Turner, *Bell*, from the *Wanted* series, 2016. Courtesy of the artists.

FIG 6 Camal Pirbhai and Camille Turner, *Bett*, from the *Wanted* series, 2016. Courtesy of the artists.

RAN away from her Master JOHN ROCK, on Monday the 18th Day of August last; a Negroe Girl named *Thursday*, about four and an half feet high, broad sett, with a Lump above her Right Eye: Had on when she run away a red Cloth Petticoat, a red Baize Bed Gown, and a red Ribbon about her Head. Whosoever may harbour said Negroe Girl, or encourage her to stay away from her said Master, may depend on being prosecuted according as the Law shall direct. And whosoever may be so kind to take her up and send her home to her said Master, shall be paid all Costs and Charges, together with TWO DOLLARS Reward for their Trouble.

JOHN ROCK.

HALIFAX, Sept. 1st, 1772.

RE-IMAGINING THE ENSLAVED

Eighteenth-Century Freedom Seekers as Twenty-First Century Sitters

CHARMAINE A. NELSON

FIG 1 Fugitive notice for Thursday, placed by John Rock of Halifax, in the *Nova Scotia Gazette and Weekly Chronicle,* September 1, 1772.

WANTED

CAMILLE TURNER *and* CAMAL PIRBHAI

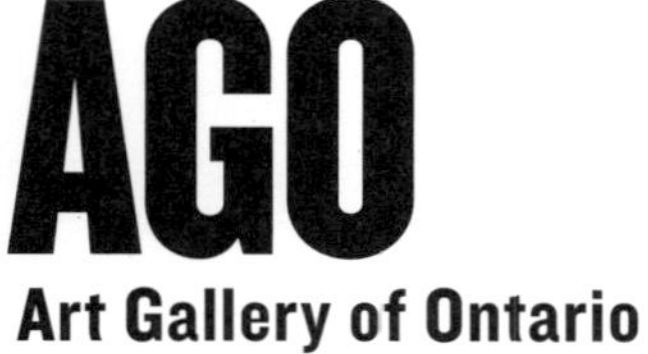

Art Gallery of Ontario